From Nomads to City Builders

History of the Aztec People Grade 4 | Children's Ancient History

First Edition, 2020

Published in the United States by Speedy Publishing LLC, 40 E Main Street, Newark, Delaware 19711 USA.

Baby Professor Books are available at special discounts when purchased in bulk for industrial and sales promotional use. For details contact our Special Sales Team at Speedy Publishing LLC, 40 E Main Street, Newark, Delaware 19711 USA. Telephone (888) 248-4521 Fax: (210) 519-4043.

10 9 8 7 6 * 5 4 3 2 1

Print Edition: 9781541953598
Digital Edition: 9781541956599
Hardcover Edition: 9781541979512

See the world in pictures. Build your knowledge in style.
www.speedypublishing.com

Table of Contents

THE AZTEC PEOPLE WENT FROM NOMADIC WANDERERS TO BUILDING SOME OF THE LARGEST CITIES IN THE WORLD.

One of the most impressive and sophisticated cultures of ancient Mesoamerica, the Aztec people flourished from about 1300 to 1521 when the empire ended in dramatic fashion. In that short time, the Aztec people went from nomadic wanderers to building some of the largest cities in the world. In this book, we will explore the history of the Aztec people from their early beginnings until the fall of the great king, Montezuma, by Spanish Conquistadors. Let's get started.

Who Were the Aztec?

The name Aztec is a variation of the old word "Aztlan", meaning "white land". Aztlan was also a term used to describe an unknown area in the northern part of Mexico. Originally a nomadic society, the Aztec did not enjoy the same longevity as their counterparts, the Olmecs and the Mayas.

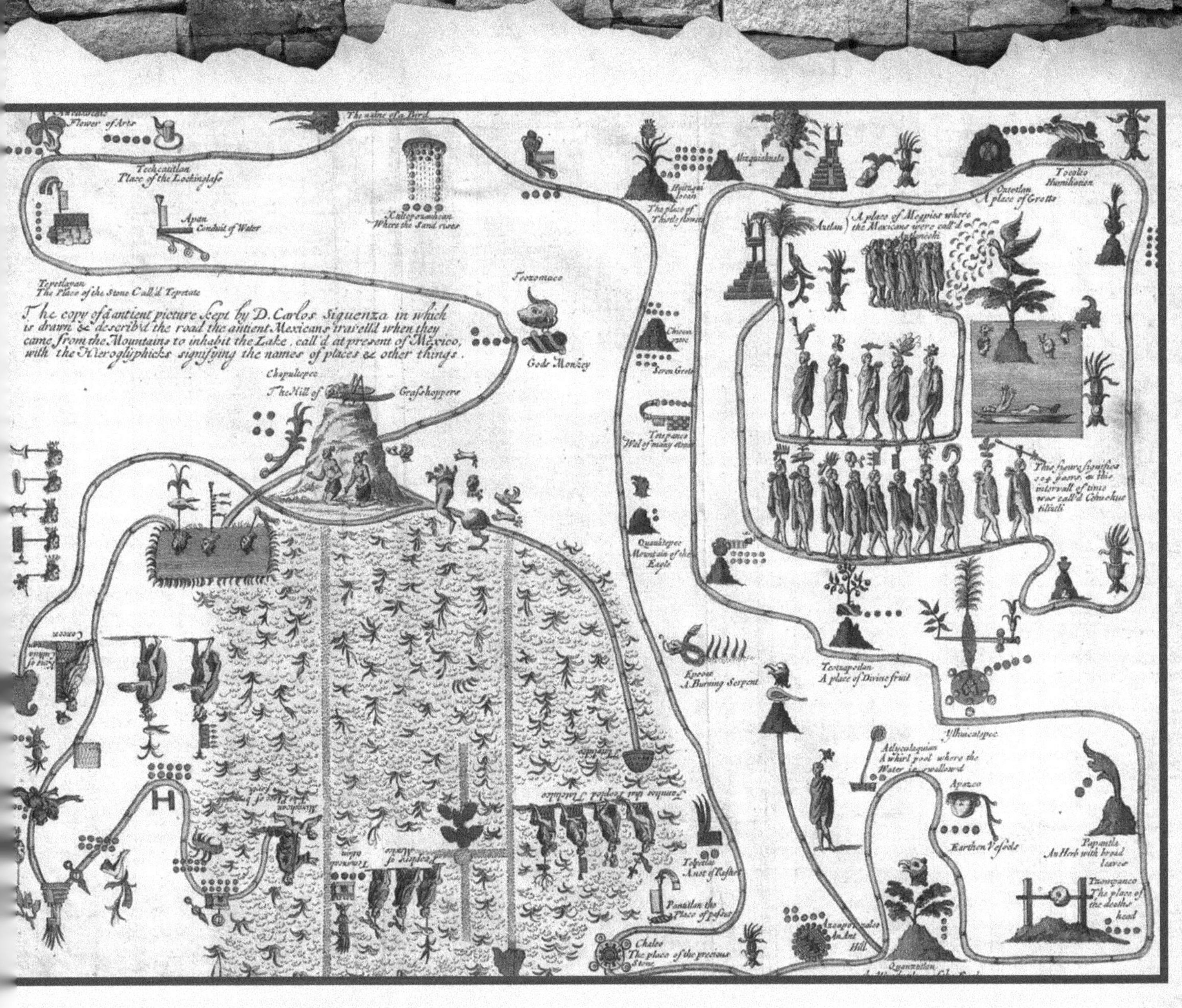

A MAP DEPICTING THE LEGENDARY AZTEC MIGRATION FROM AZTLAN, A MYSTERIOUS PARADISE SOMEWHERE TO THE NORTHWEST OF MEXICO, TO CHAPULTEPEC HILL, CURRENTLY MEXICO CITY.

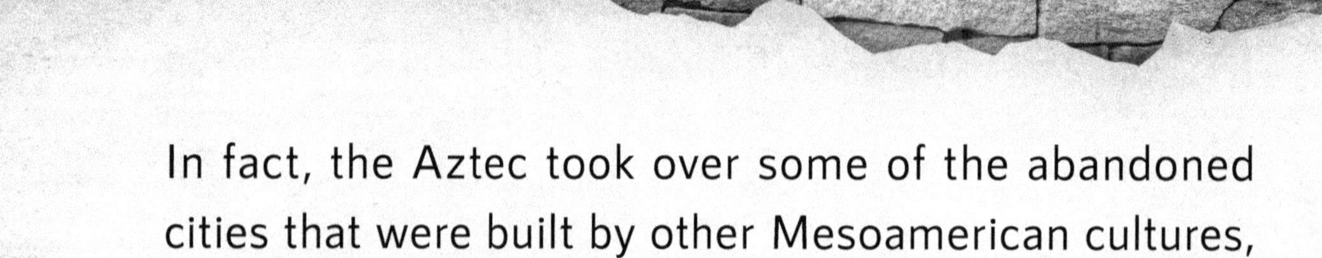

In fact, the Aztec took over some of the abandoned cities that were built by other Mesoamerican cultures, including the sprawling capital city of Teotihuacan in what is now central Mexico.

GENERAL VIEW OF THE RUINS IN TEOTIHUACAN, MEXICO

Before the Aztec

Before the Aztec came on the scene, Mesoamerica was home to several significant cultures upon which the Aztecs built their empire. The oldest known Mesoamerican society was the Olmec. This group of people date back to as far as 1200 BC. Not much is known about the Olmec, but they did leave behind a collection of giant stone heads that have puzzled archaeologists.

OLMEC COLOSSAL HEAD IN LA VENTA PARK, VILLAHERMOSA, TABASCO, MEXICO

After the decline of the Olmecs, the Zapotec people thrived in the region from about 500 BC to 1000 AD.

RUINS OF THE ANCIENT CITY OF THE ANCIENT MESOAMERICAN ZAPOTEC CIVILIZATION OF MONTE ALBAN IN OAXACA, MEXICO.

In addition, the Mayas ruled parts of what is now Mexico from 1000 BC to 1521 AD.

A MURAL PAINTING OF ANCIENT MAYA CIVILIZATION.

The Mixtec culture existed from about 900 to 1521 AD, and the Aztec empire flourished between 1200 and 1521 AD. You may have noticed that three of the Mesoamerican cultures ended in the same year, 1521 AD. We will discuss the circumstances of this date in a moment.

DETAIL FROM THE CODEX ZOUCHE-NUTTALL, DEPICTING THE LIFE OF THE MIXTEC RULER EIGHT DEER JAGUAR-CLAW (RIGHT).

Aztec Nomads

Early in their existence, the Aztec people lived a nomadic lifestyle. They followed animal migrations to keep their food supply abundant. According to their own written stories, the Aztec people wandered the region for hundreds of years, searching for just the right spot to build their great city. Legend told them that they would know they had found the right place when they saw a serpent and an eagle fighting on a cactus. This would be the sign that they were in the place they were destined to be.

AZTEC PRIESTS DISCOVERING THE SPOT WHERE AN EAGLE,
DEVOURING A SERPENT, SITS ATOP A CACTUS.

Aztec Farmers

In time, however, they learned farming practices and became experts in agriculture. They learned how to carve terraces into steep hills to make flat farmland. They developed irrigation systems and found ways to drain swamps to make more farmland. They even designed a way to construct artificial islands within the natural lakes, all to help them maximize cultivation.

AZTECS DESIGNED A WAY TO CONSTRUCT ARTIFICIAL ISLANDS WITHIN THE NATURAL LAKES TO HELP THEM MAXIMIZE CULTIVATION.

Mesoamerican farmers used crossbreeding techniques to transform a grass-like plant into corn, or maize, the most important food crop in the region. In addition to corn and beans, the Aztec farmers grew tomatoes, squash, tobacco, peppers, and cotton.

MESOAMERICAN FARMERS USED CROSSBREEDING TECHNIQUES TO TRANSFORM A GRASS-LIKE PLANT INTO CORN.

The Aztec Religion

The Aztec people had a complex religion with numerous gods. Each god represented some aspect of nature and controlled that realm. The Aztecs went to great lengths to keep their gods happy so that the forces of the natural world would remain in balance with each other. To appease the gods, they practiced human sacrifice. They thought that by giving the gods the precious gift of human life, they would be making the gods very happy.

AN AZTEC PRIEST OFFERING A HUMAN SACRIFICE TO APPEASE THE GODS.

Most of the people killed during the ritualistic human sacrifices were either prisoners of war or were slaves. It has been estimated that thousands of people were sacrificed to the Aztec gods. Among the more important gods in the Aztec pantheon were the sun god Huitzilopochtli and the god of death Quetzalcoatl.

AN ILLUSTRATION OF AZTEC MYTHICAL GOD HUITZILOPOCHTLI, GOD OF SUN AND WAR

AN ILLUSTRATION OF AZTEC MYTHICAL GOD QUETZALCOATL, GOD OF DEATH

The Aztec Empire

As a small, nomadic group, the Aztec were in constant conflict with neighboring groups. But their numbers increased, as well as their military and political power.

RANKS OF WARRIORS IN THE AZTEC ARMY

Around 1200 AD, as their population grew, they moved into the central part of Mexico and absorbed aspects of the legends, heritages, and cultures of the previous civilizations that thrived there. The Aztecs settled on the islands in a large lake, Lake Texcoco, presumably because they encountered an eagle and a snake battling each other on a cactus at this spot.

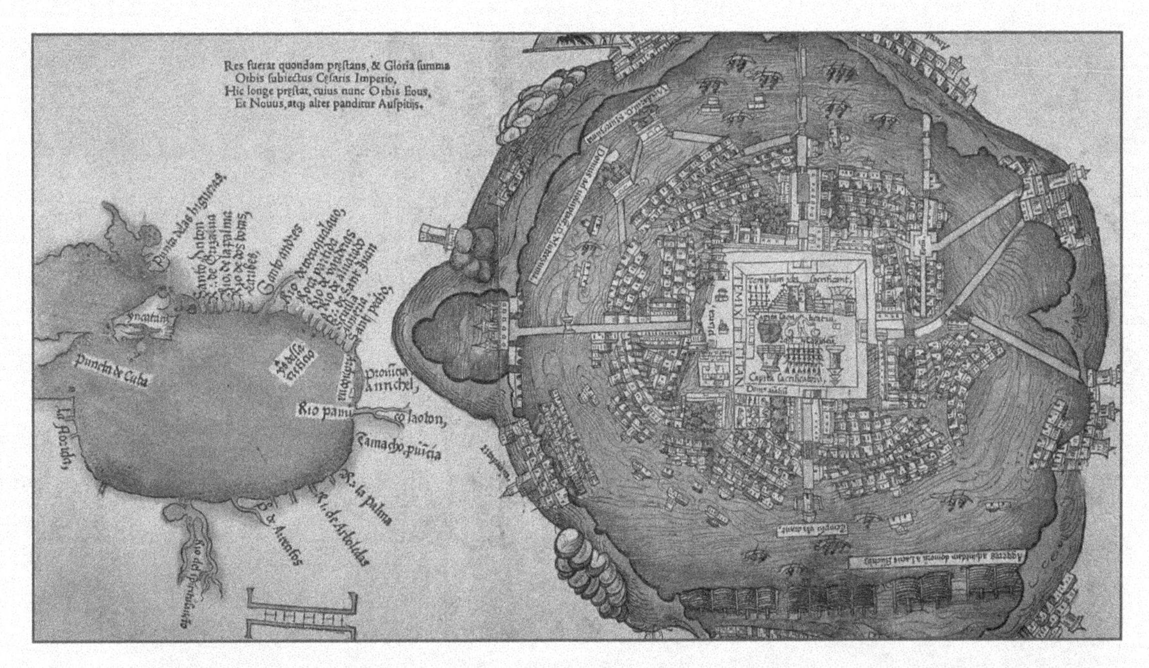

LAKE TEXCOCO IS BEST KNOWN AS WHERE THE AZTECS BUILT THE CITY OF TENOCHTITLAN, WHICH WAS LOCATED ON AN ISLAND WITHIN THE LAKE.

Aztec City Builders

With their experience as island builders, the Aztec were able to expand the natural islands of the lake to build their great city, Tenochtitlan. Construction on the city was completed around 1325 AD. The city was a showcase of the wealth and prestige that the Aztec had acquired.

CONSTRUCTION OF TENOCHTITLAN.

The buildings were made with stone and clay. The city had soaring pyramids, shining palaces, and sacred temples. There were canals and aqueducts for the transportation of water. The city boasted elaborate gardens and even a zoo. Lake Texcoco, in which Tenochtitlan was built, was later drained as the modern-day capital city, Mexico City was erected on the site.

RECONSTRUCTED CENTRAL TENOCHTITLÁN SQUARE AND TEMPLO MAYOR.

The Triple Alliance

Tenochtitlan wasn't the only Aztec city. The leaders of Tenochtitlan joined forces with the people of two other important Aztec cities, Texcoco and Tlacopan, around 1426. This alliance of the three most powerful cities in central Mexico gave the Aztecs even more control over the region.

AZTEC GLYPHS FOR THE MEMBER-STATES OF THE AZTEC TRIPLE ALLIANCE: TEXCOCO (LEFT), TENOCHTITLAN (MIDDLE), AND TLACOPAN (RIGHT).

Although the Triple Alliance shared the power, the leaders of each city held the title of emperor, or huetlatoani. The Triple Alliance controlled the region for more than a century and brought several other cities under their authority.

ITZCOATL WAS THE FOURTH KING OF TENOCHTITLAN, AND FIRST EMPEROR OF THE AZTEC EMPIRE RULING FROM 1427 TO 1440.

NEZAHUALCOYOTL WAS THE RULER OF THE CITY-STATE OF TEXCOCO.

TOTOQUIHUAZTLI WAS THE FIRST RULER OF TLACOPAN.

These cities maintained their **autonomy**[1] but were required to pay taxes to the Triple Alliance. In return, they received the backing of the mighty army of the three allies. It was an **amicable**[2] arrangement that allowed the Aztec Empire to grow to encompass an area of more than 115,000 square miles.

1 Autonomy – Freedom and independence
2 Amicable – Friendly and peacefully

The Aztec Language

The spoken language of the Aztec people was called Nahua. Later, after the Aztecs were defeated by Spain, Spanish became the dominant language of the region. Numerous Aztec words were adopted into the Spanish language and, from there, made their way into English. Coyote, tomato, chocolate, and avocado were all originally Nahua words spoken by the Aztecs. The Aztec people did not have a written language with an alphabet. To communicate, they used a system of pictograms and **glyphs**[3], with pictures and images to represent words or ideas.

3 Glyphs – Pictures, images, or heirglyphics

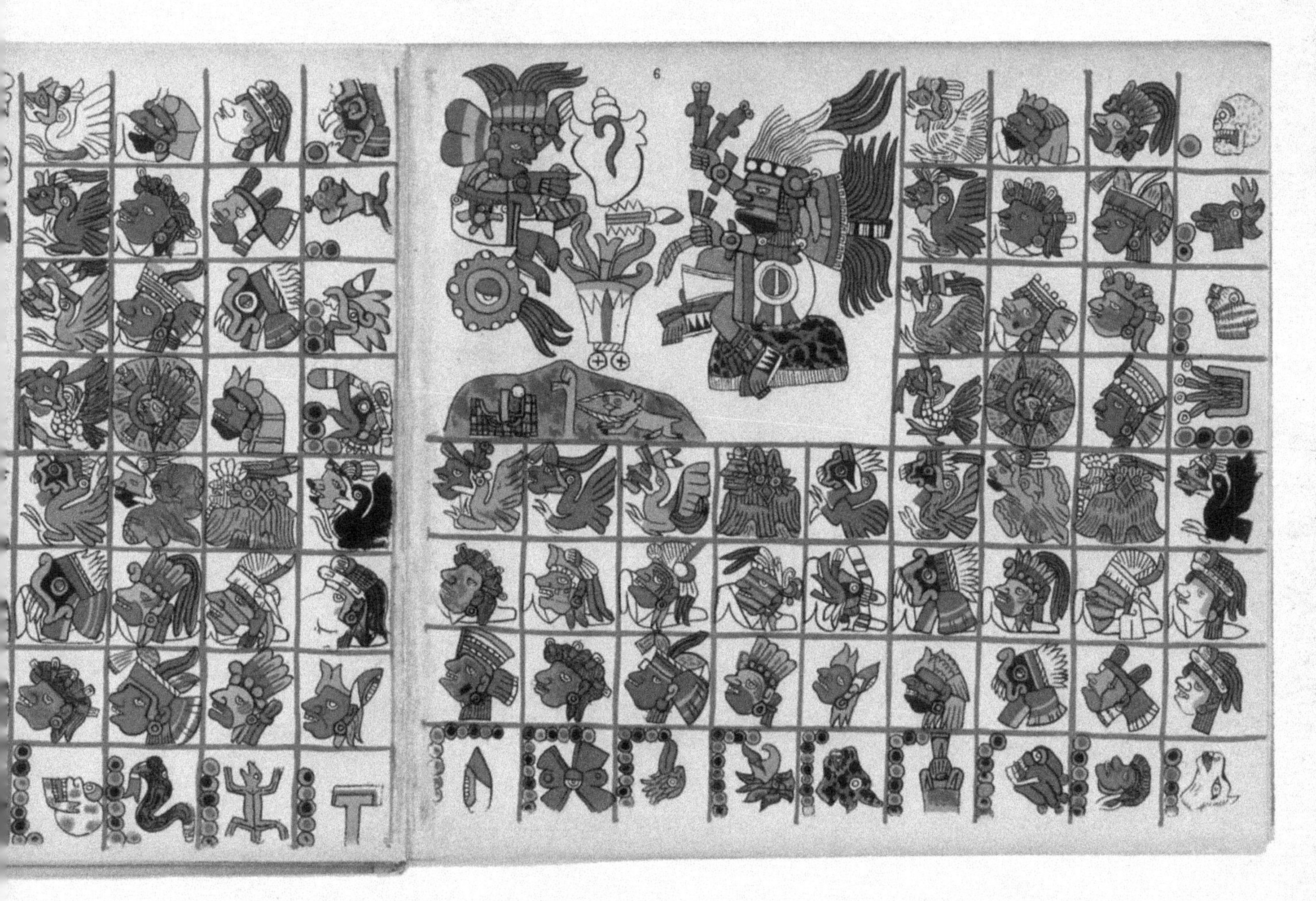

THE AZTECS FOLLOWED A SIMPLE WRITING SYSTEM MADE UP OF PICTOGRAMS.

Aztec Kings

Several years after establishing their central city at Tenochtitlan, the Aztec people chose their first king. Acamapichtli was selected as the first Aztec king, or tlatoani. He presided over the government, military, and religious rituals of the Aztec and worked to establish alliances with neighboring tribes.

ACAMAPICHTLI

The role of the Aztec king expanded, and, in time, the people began to believe that the king was a divine leader, a descendant of the great gods themselves. The eighth Aztec king, Ahuitzotl, took the title of huey tlatoani, meaning "supreme king". Under his rule, which ended in 1502, the Aztec Empire reached its largest size. Ahuitzoti's successor was Montezuma, the last Aztec king.

AHUITZOTL

Montezuma

When Montezuma II ascended to the Aztec throne in 1503, the Aztec Empire included roughly 6 million people. The empire was at its peak in terms of wealth, power, and size, but it all came crashing down.

MONTEZUMA II

QUETZALCOATL

The Aztec legends claimed that the god, Quetzalcoatl, represented by the feathered serpent, would return from his banishment across the sea and bring profound changes to the Aztec way of life.

The Aztec priests, using the complex calendar system that the Aztec adopted from the Mayans, predicted that Quetzalcoatl would return in the year 1519, during the reign of Montezuma. Knowing this prediction explains Montezuma's response to the invading Spanish Conquistadors.

ANCIENT AZTEC CALENDAR

Cortez and the Conquistadors

A strange event did take place in 1519, just as the Aztec priests predicted, but it wasn't the triumphant return of Quetzalcoatl. It was the arrival of Hernan Cortes, an explorer from Spain. Cortes and his men arrived on the shores of what is now Mexico in 1519. The Aztec people had never before seen such large ships with enormous white sails.

HERNAN CORTES

CORTES WAS WELCOMED INTO THE AZTEC CAPITAL OF TENOCHTITLAN.

The Spaniards had with them horses and they road atop them ... another astonishing sight for the native people. Montezuma thought that Cortes must be the returning god, Quetzalcoatl, so he presented him with gifts of elaborate foods, gold, jade jewelry, and even a robe made from the feathers of colorful parrots. Cortes was welcomed into the Aztec capital of Tenochtitlan.

The Fall of the Aztecs

Hernan Cortes was impressed with the riches of Tenochtitlan. He plotted to take their gold and jewels for Spain. There were far more Aztec warriors than there were Spanish Conquistadors, but Cortes and his men had something that the Aztec had never seen ... guns. With their superior weaponry, Cortes and his men seized Tenochtitlan and imprisoned Montezuma.

HERNAN CORTES TAKES MONTEZUMA II AS PRISONER.

THE PEOPLE WERE APPALLED BY MONTEZUMA'S COMPLICITY AND PELTED HIM WITH ROCKS.

The Aztec king still believed that Cortes was the **prophesized**[4] god and was therefore unwilling to order his armies to fight against him. As the Spanish continued to rule the city, most of the Aztec people grew frustrated with their leader. When Cortes brought Montezuma out of his cell to calm his people, the Aztec responded by **pelting**[5] their emperor with rocks. Montezuma was gravely injured and died a few days later.

---

4 Prophesized – Predicting the future
5 Pelting – Throwing with force

The Fall of Tenochtitlan

Until now, Cortes had kept control of Tenochtitlan without resorting to too much violence. Instead, he used fear. But after the death of Montezuma, the Aztec people drove Cortes and his men from the city. They regrouped and plotted to retake the city. In May of 1521, they attacked. With guns and canons, the Spaniards were able to defeat the Aztecs.

AZTEC SOLDIERS OVERWHELMED CORTES' FORCES TENOCHTITLAN AND DROVE THEM FROM THE CITY

They destroyed the great city, stole its riches, and toppled its temples. The year 1521 marked the end of the Aztec Empire, as well as other Mesoamerican cultures. After that, the Spanish colonized the region and almost completely wiped out traces of the once-great Aztec civilization.

THE CONQUEST OF TENOCHTITLAN BY THE SPANISH ARMY OF HERNANDO CORTES.

Summary

The Aztec culture came on the heels of other great Mesoamerican civilizations, including the Toltec, Olmec, and Mayan, but in the short time that they controlled central Mexico, they built a great empire with a large, prosperous city at its center. Religion was a major factor in the lives of the Aztec people, which was why, when the Spanish Conquistadors led by Hernan Cortes arrived in 1519, the Aztec king, Montezuma, viewed the event as the return of an important god. Even though they were drastically outnumbered, the Spanish defeated the Aztec and destroyed their great city, ending the Aztec society.

Visit

www.speedypublishing.com

To view and download free content on your favorite subject and browse our catalog of new and exciting books for readers of all ages.

Lightning Source UK Ltd.
Milton Keynes UK
UKHW051250060121
376517UK00002B/41